A Book of Welsh Bakestone Cookery

traditional recipes from the country kitchens of Wales
by
Bobby Freeman

y Lolfa

'Put the baking-stone
on, will you? I will
make milk cakes for supper.'

Richard Llewellyn: 'How Green was my Valley'.

The ancient bakestone is an everyday survival in the Wales of today. In town and country alike, cooks proudly admit to its regular use—and what they mean is an old, heavy, black cast-iron one which has perhaps been in the family for generations, not some new-fangled special-surfaced griddle unit, although 'griddle' is what the bakestone is likely to be called elsewhere. In Welsh it has several names according to region and meaning—*planc, maen, llechfaen, gradell,* hence *bara planc* (bakestone bread), *pice ar y maen* (cakes on the bakestone).

Gradell is the north and mid Wales term and means 'an iron plate to make cakes upon'. *Planc* is the Welsh synonym for plank—'an iron plank for the baking of bread' and is the term used in west Wales and part of what was Breconshire. In the old county of Glamorgan the terms were *maen* (stone) for an actual stone bakestone, and *llechfaen* for what was literally a slate-stone, common to some parts of the south and south-west.

The portable stone, and then iron, bakestone was the follow-on from the early, primitive method of baking on a hot hearth or flagstone, which had first developed as a thin slab built into a wall with room for a fire beneath. Thus 'bakestone', or as Richard Llewellyn had it, 'baking-stone', is the literal meaning.

Baking bread on a hot stone with an iron pot inverted over a dough was a Celtic innovation which gave the bread a little rise. This ancient practice continued in remote parts of Wales into the early years of this century, using the iron bakestone with a slow-burning fire beneath and smouldering coals heaped on top, obtaining a much better result from proper bread yeast in the dough instead of the wild yeasts of the air which the Celts were attempting to assist by the steam from this enclosed method of baking.

A heavy black frying pan substitutes perfectly if a bakestone cannot be obtained, but they are being made again and can be bought in craft shops in Wales. Judge the heat by holding your hand just above the surface—experience will be your guide. A well-proven bakestone needs almost no grease. It all depends on what you are cooking—mixtures with sugar in them require the greatest care—and grease.

Probably the bakestone is most famous in Wales for the ubiquitous Welsh cakes. Nowadays housewives literally get the best of both worlds by baking big batches on the bakestone and then storing them in the freezer. But in Wales there are many, many quickly-made cakes and breads for the bakestone, of which pancakes are perhaps the most enduringly popular. They could be whipped off the bakestone at a moment's notice for the unexpected visitor; they were, and still are, a birthday treat.

When pancakes were on the menu on Shrove Tuesday in an industrial canteen in west Wales, I was amazed to see an old bakestone come out of its cupboard to be placed over a couple of bricks set either side of one of the gas burners on the vast cooking range. On this, amid the gleaming steel and steam of contemporary catering equipment, the cook stood patiently making pancake after pancake, hour after hour, until the men's demands for them were appeased.

What characterises Welsh pancakes is that they are made in a pile, well buttered, then cut down in wedges and eaten like a cake. They have many names in Welsh: *crempog* is general in north Wales and Ceredigion; *ffroesen* in the south; *pancogen* and *pancosen* in the west and south-west and *cramwythen* in the south-west. They have brothers and sisters called lightcakes and batter cakes.

The *slapan* (batter cake) is another extension of the pancake, this time baked thick on the bakestone, then split and buttered.

The lightcakes (*leicecs*) of Wales are similar to Scottish drop scones, but often made with buttermilk. They are particularly associated with Denbigh and Merionnydd, and at a 500 year-old hill farm high above Aberdyfi, where the fire was still 'on the floor' and the 50 year-old daughter of the household was famous for her lightcakes, I learned that the farm had for generations been noted for the quality of these delicious bakestone treats. Long ago, I was told, the young men of the district would walk out from Aberdyfi to the farm of an evening to vie with each other as to how many *leicecs* each could consume: remembering the precipitous climb up to the old farm which my little car had almost refused, I realise how good those *leicecs* must have been to have lured those young men upwards on foot.

Recollecting my Lancashire childhood boasts of Shrove Tuesday pancake consumption, the universality of pancake-eating contest is apparent: remember Little Black Sambo who ate 169?

BAKESTONE
(planc, maen, llechfaen, gradell)

Welsh Cakes
Pice ar y maen

There are two ways of making these traditional little
spicy cakes, and by far the most usual is the bakestone.
But they do need to be eaten while they are warm and
fresh and made from a rich enough mixture to prevent a
dry, biscuity result.

The other method is in a Dutch oven, which from the
same mixture produces cakes which are firm on the
outside, soft and melting within. Baking under a medium
grill gives similar results.

8 ozs SR flour and ½ teas. baking powder
4 ozs butter, margarine
3 ozs sugar
3 ozs currants
1 large egg and a little milk
good pinch mixed spice or just nutmeg
METRIC: 225g flour; 125g butter; 75g sugar; 75g currants

Rub the fat into the spiced flour (butter for a traditional
taste!), add the sugar and currants, bind with beaten egg
and a little milk if needed to a stiffish paste—similar to
shortcrust but a little softer. Roll out on a floured board
to about ¼in thick, cut into 2½in rounds and bake on a
greased, moderately hot bakestone, 3-5 mins each side
until mottled with golden brown. Sprinkle with sugar.

The Quire of Quire Paper

This was a fashionable novelty in the 18th century, a *must* for the hostess in the great house, including those of Wales as the MS cookery books found in Welsh mansions confirm. The quire consisted of 20 pancakes in a pile, representing the old measure of paper.

The pancakes were a rich mixture of cream, flavoured with sherry and rosewater or orange-flower water, and nutmeg, and they were literally as thin as paper. The pile when complete was cut down in wedges to serve.

4 ozs plain flour
2 eggs and 2 yolks
½ pint single cream or Jersey milk
2 tbls. caster sugar
2 tbls. sweet sherry + dash of rosewater or orange-flower water
4 ozs butter, melted
½ grated nutmeg
METRIC: 125g flour and butter; 275mls (10 fl. ozs) cream

Make the batter in the usual way, adding the melted, cooled butter last. This will solidify in the batter, but it will melt upon contact with the hot pan, so just grease it lightly for the first pancake. Use an omlette pan and make the pancakes paperthin—they will be fragile at the edges so ease them gently before turning with a knife.

Sprinkle each with sugar as you build the 'quire'.

Lightcakes
Leicecs

These should be small 3-4 ins across at most. Some
recipes do indicate a larger size, but as the bakestone
cannot easily be tilted they are difficult to handle. They
are best made with buttermilk.

4 ozs plain flour
3 ozs sugar
1 egg
¼ teas. bicarb. soda
pinch salt
buttermilk, or milk to mix
METRIC: 125g flour; 75g sugar

Mix the dry ingredients in a bowl. If using buttermilk,
dissolve the bicarb. soda in this, then beat up with the
egg. Pour this mixture in a well in the centre of the flour
etc. and beat to a thick, creamy batter. Drop on to a
hot, well-greased bakestone. Turn when bubbles appear
on the top surface and the underneath is golden brown.
Serve warm with butter.

Speckled Cake
Cacen Gri

This stiffish mixture is usually made as one cake on the bakestone, but according to Lloyd George's housekeeper, Dame Margaret made small thin rounds, piling them on top of each other with plenty of salty Welsh butter spread between. It was one of Lloyd George's special favourites.

1 lb plain flour
6 ozs butter
1 egg
a few currants
1 teas. each baking powder and bicarb. soda
sugar to taste, milk to mix
METRIC: 450g flour; 175g butter

Mix the raising agents into the flour and rub in the butter. Add currants and sugar. Beat the egg into the milk and mix into the flour etc. Roll out thinly and bake on a well-greased bakestone.

(from 'Lloyd George's Favourite Dishes')

David's Batter Cake
Slapan Dafydd

An Anglesey recipe.

10 ozs plain flour
2 ozs butter
3 ozs sugar
3 ozs sultanas
2 eggs
½ pint warmed buttermilk
1 tbls. vinegar
1 teas. bicarbonate soda
½ teas. salt
METRIC: 275g flour; 50g butter; 75g each sugar and sultanas 275mls (10 fl. ozs) buttermilk

Put the flour, salt and sultanas in a bowl. Melt the butter in the warm buttermilk, then gradualy pour into the dry mixture and beat well. Leave to stand a few hours if possible.

Beat the eggs, add sugar, soda and vinegar and pour this second mixture into the first, beating well.

Pour on to a moderately hot bakestone to make one large cake. Turn when golden on the under side. Split in half while warm and spread with butter to serve.

Light Cake of Gwent & Glamorgan
Teisen frau Gwent a Morgannwg

from Lady Llanover's 'Good Cookery' 1867

Two versions are given, one to be baked in a Dutch oven, this one for the bakestone. The author recommends sheep's milk cream, but in the likely absence of this, use cow's milk cream.

> '*A variety of the Teisen Frau are* (sic) *made by rubbing six ounces of butter in one pound of flour and two teaspoonfuls of sugar made into a stiff dough with new milk, or sheep's-milk cream; roll it out half an inch thick, and cut to size required; bake on a bakestone . . .*'

Note: I have baked this mixture as one cake, in the oven, and successfully used it for a fruit shortcake.

Bakestone Turnovers
Teisennau ar y Maen

It took me a long time to make these successfully, while I was trying to make them as in this picture—a circle of shortcrust folded over. Then I went to Plas Glansevin near Llandeilo, where these scrumptious little fruit tarts are a speciality of the hotel's famous Welsh teas. There they are made in rounds, 4-5 ins. across, and in this way the top pastry is easier to lift off for the brown sugar and butter to be worked into the hot fruit before serving with whipped cream. It is this butter and sugar treatment which gives the turnovers their characteristic appeal.

1 lb plain flour
6 ozs butter, or margarine
cooked apple, rhubarb or other fruit
brown molasses sugar
butter
METRIC: 450g flour; 175g butter or margarine

Drain the cooked fruit really well and cool. Place on small pastry rounds, damp the edges, cover with another round and pinch the edges tightly together. Cook gently on both sides on a moderate bakestone until mottled with gold. Trim the edge and ease the lid off with a sharp knife. Work sugar and butter into the fruit, close the turnover and serve at once with whipped cream.

Note: made as one large turnover and afterwards cut into squares, this was known as Harvest Cake.

Crab Cake
Teisen Afal Surion Bach

This recipe was given to me by Mrs Davies of Colwilston in the Vale of Glamorgan—one of the few areas in Wales where crabapples grow—it is the jelly from this fruit which gives the cake its name.

1 lb SR flour
4 ozs butter or margarine
6 ozs caster sugar
2 large eggs
pinch salt, nutmeg
METRIC: 450g flour; 125g butter; 175g sugar

Rub fat into flour, add sugar, salt and nutmeg. Make into a stiff dough with the beaten egg, roll out into two plate-size rounds. Spread one with crabapple jelly, cover and seal egdes tightly. To make this successfully you need a wooden paddle like the one in the picture on p. 14 otherwise the cake is impossible to turn in one piece. But it can be made as smaller cakes.

Quick-mix Cake
Teisen Ffwrdd a Hi

8 ozs plain flour
2 ozs butter
2 ozs sugar
2 ozs currants
pinch salt, milk to mix
METRIC: 225g flour; 50g each butter, sugar, currants

Rub the butter into the flour, add the other dry
ingredients. Mix with milk to a stiffish mixture which
will spread evenly over a moderately hot, greased
bakestone.

Bake on both sides until golden, then split while still
warm and spread with butter to serve.

Tinker's Cake
Teisen Dinca

Whether this cake was made in honour of the travelling tinker who was welcomed for his repairs to pans and kettles, or whether he contrived it himself as a quick camp-fire bake I am not able to say. But there is no doubt about its rich goodness. Don't economise on the brown sugar!

1 lb plain flour
8 ozs butter
6 ozs light molasses sugar
8 ozs grated cooking apple
milk or beaten egg to mix
pinch salt
METRIC: 450g flour; 225g butter; 125g sugar; 225g apple

Rub the butter into the flour, mix in the apple, sugar and salt. Bind with milk or beaten egg to a fairly stiff dough. Roll out to rounds ⅓ of an inch thick. Bake on a moderately hot bakestone, 3 or 4 mins. each side. Sprinkle with sugar to serve.

Green Pancake
Crempog Las

This interesting savoury pancake was doubtless intended,
like Yorkshire pudding, as a 'stretcher' for the main dish
of meat. But it is tasty enough to eat by itself, or with
grilled bacon or sausages.

8 ozs flour (450g)
2 eggs
chopped fresh parsley
chopped shallot or spring onion
pepper and salt
milk to mix

Make a stiff batter with the flour, milk and eggs—much
stiffer than for pancakes. Stir in the very finely-chopped
onions and parsley. Cook gently on a moderate
bakestone on both sides, taking care not to let the
outside burn or the inside remain uncooked. Spread with
butter to serve.

Yeast Pancakes
Crempog Furum

Unlike ordinary pancakes, yeast pancakes do not run, but sit firmly in little heaps, which makes them very suitable for the bakestone which has the disadvantage of being impossible to tilt.

12 ozs plain flour (or strong bread flour)
¼ oz yeast
2 small eggs
3 tbls. sugar
large knob butter
pinch salt
½ pint milk or buttermilk
METRIC: 350g flour; 12g yeast, 10g butter; 425mls (15fl. ozs) milk

Cream the yeast with a little sugar. Warm the milk and melt the butter in it. Add sugar and salt to the flour in a bowl, make a well in the centre and pour in the beaten egg. Gradually add the milk and beat to a smooth batter. Lastly, add the creamed yeast and set aside in a warm place to rise.

Bake as small pancakes and split them in half and butter generously to serve.

Oatcakes
Bara Ceirch

In Wales, oatcakes were most often made on the bakestone, but sometimes on the iron shelves of an oven, when a special wooden paddle (*crafell*) was used for putting them in and taking them out.

Welsh oatcakes traditionally were huge—'big as dinner-plates' is a recurring comparison, then and now—and thin to the point of transparency. Making them was a skilled operation, as I found to my chagrin. Having failed to 'palm' mine to more than 8 inches across, I went, humbly, to Lampeter, to watch 95-year-old Mrs Davies make them 10 inches across at least. Without the aid of a rolling pin or anything other than her deft hands, she worked a pile of spreading oatcakes under each hand simultaneously, growing larger by the minute, the edges kept firm by an alternating up-ending rolling on the table, dexteriously held in pairs between her palms. Hard to describe—I was grateful for the lesson, but no better at achieving that splendid size.

Take Mrs Davies' daughter's advice (who cannot achieve the size either) and cravenly fall back on the use of that modern gadget—the rolling pin.

Whichever way they are to be flattened, the oatmeal is kneaded first with skim milk or water, or as in the second recipe, with a little bacon fat, or vegetable oil, until it holds together as a dough. This is quite hard work and takes up to 10 minutes.

It is essential to use the correct medium grade of oatmeal —too coarse a meal and the dough will not hold properly, too fine and it will be sticky.

22

Break the dough off in balls and flatten them on an oatmeal-strewn board. Sprinkle oatmeal on top and add another flattened ball. Continue to make in as big a pile as you can manage until the oatcakes are as large and thin as possible, holding the edges firm by working against a cupped hand.

Bake on a medium bakestone, or on a baking sheet in a medium oven. Usually on the bakestone the oatcakes were cooked on one side only, then placed standing-up with the unbaked side towards the fire. They kept for months in an air-tight container: often a whole day would be set aside for baking them in Mrs Davies' day.

The use of the word *bara* (bread) and not *cacen* or *teisen* (cake) in the Welsh is indicative of their importance as a staple bread in Wales.

Recipe 1

Medium-grade oatmeal, quantity depending upon how many oatcakes you wish to make, say 1 lb. Skim milk or water to mix.

Put the oatmeal in a bowl, moisten with milk or water and mix with a wooden spoon initally. When a dough is formed, knead with the hands, adding more liquid until the dough feels pliable. Then proceed to make the oatcakes as described.

Oatcakes

Recipe 2

4 tablespoons medium oatmeal
½ tablespoons bacon fat or oil
3 tablespoons hot water
pinch salt

These small quantities are explained by the advisability of mixing and rolling out only a few oatcakes at a time, before the mixture hardens. This is the recipe I prefer.

Heat the fat in the water. Sprinkle the oatmeal on to it, kneading well. Flour a board with oatmeal, roll the dough out very thinly to about 10 inches in diameter if you can manage it. Bake for about 5-10 minutes on a moderately hot bakestone, one side only. Stand up against the fire to harden the other side.

Pikelets
Bara Pyglyd

1 lb plain strong white flour
1 teas. dried yeast
½ pint milk with ½ pint water mixed
1 desserts. sea salt
1 teas. sugar
2 tbls. oil
METRIC: 450g flour; 275mls milk and 275mls water

The English name is thought to be a corruption of the
Welsh. 'Pitchy bread' was another name for these yeast
pancakes which resemble the thicker English crumpet
(cooked in rings) in their mixture. But most of the more
recent recipes in Wales have become muddled with the
pancake and lightcake recipes and are egg and soda
mixes. The Welsh love holey griddle breads and cakes,
for the holes ar capable of holding so much lovely golden
butter.

Warm flour in low oven 5 mins. Warm oil, milk/water,
sugar to blood heat—use a little to cream the yeast. Add
salt to warmed flour, make a batter with the yeasty
liquid. Beat it very well until quite smooth. Cover bowl
and leave to rise at room temperature 1½-2 hours until
well up the bowl and covered with bubbles. Beat down
with a spoon, cover again and leave to recover 30 mins.
in a warm place. Cook pikelets one at a time (about
6 ins. across) on a lightly-greased moderately hot
bakestone. The holes appear very quickly. Cook both sides
to a pale brown colour.

Bakestone Bread
Bara Planc

1 lb plain white strong flour
½ teas. sea salt
1 teas. bicarbonate of soda
½ pint buttermilk
METRIC: 450g plain flour; 275mls buttermilk

The bakestone was often pressed into service to make a quick loaf, sometimes with a yeast dough taken from the main batch on baking day, but equally often with a dough employing another raising agent, as in this recipe which I find easier to manage on the bakestone than a yeast dough. The ability to make a quick loaf on the bakestone is a useful acquisition, but it is not easy, and mastering the knack a salutory lesson in appreciating the skills of earlier cooks.

Add the salt to the flour, dissolve the soda in the buttermilk and mix gradually into the flour to form a soft dough. Knead lightly and turn on to a floured board. Shape into a round, flattening the top with a rolling pin. The bakestone must be well greased and not too hot or the loaf will burn on the outside before it is done inside. Cook both sides to a golden brown.

In this series
1. A Book of Welsh Bread
2. A Book of Welsh Country Cakes and Buns
3. A Book of Welsh Bakestone Cookery
4. A Book of Welsh Country Puddings and Pies
5. A Book of Welsh Fish
6. A Book of Welsh Soups and Savouries

Also by Bobby Freeman
Lloyd George's Favourite Dishes (1974, 1976, 1978 – Ed.)
Gwent – A Guide to South East Wales (1980)
First Catch Your Peacock – A Book of Welsh Food (1980)
Welsh Country House Cookery (1983)
Welsh Country Cookery – Traditional Recipes from the
Country Kitchens of Wales (Y Lolfa, 1987)

First impression: 1984
Sixth impression: 2006

© Bobby Freeman 1984
ISBN 0 86243 139 5

Printed and published in Wales by
Y Lolfa Cyf., Talybont, Ceredigion SY24 5AP
tel (01970) 832304   *fax* 832782
email ylolfa@ylolfa.com   *web* www.ylolfa.com

Please send for our free full-colour catalogue!